# LADAKH

# LADAKH

## Between Earth and Sky

Text by Siddiq Wahid
Photographs by Kenneth R. Storm, Jr.

W.W. Norton & Company

NEW YORK AND LONDON

This book was created and produced by Edita S.A. Lausanne

# Table of Contents

# Acknowledgements

*We should like to take this opportunity to thank Mr. Roger Du Pasquier who first suggested the book to us and so kindly helped us in getting it published. Our thanks are due also to Ghafoor Wahid, who travelled with photographer Kenneth Storm on his journeys in Ladakh and greatly enhanced his understanding of the land and its people; to Alok Chandola, to whom the author of the text owes his improved views on tourism; and to Mountain Travel India, who bore part of the expenses for our project.*

*To our parents*
*S.W.*
*K.S.*

# Introduction

Ladakh possesses an appeal which considerably predates 1974, the year in which it was opened to international tourism; those few westerners who had previously visited the country had already remarked upon its austere yet exhilarating character. Of course, they rarely achieved a profound understanding of the people and their culture, more often demonstrating the condescending attitude so typical of colonial era Europeans. But however strong their tendency to misunderstand the inhabitants of that far-off land, they were rarely indifferent to its peaceful majesty, and its lack of contamination by modern civilization. Not a few travellers were sensible of a mysterious presence of the sublime.

Those who had had the privilege of visiting Ladakh before the war – we have encountered a few – invariably speak with emotion of their penetration into an exquisitely cohesive world where men's lives unfolded according to nature's rhythm and in harmony with the serene grandeur of the Himalayan landscape. At that time, any westerner, even an Englishman, wishing to go to Ladakh was obliged to obtain special permission, generally granted, from the British Resident in Srinagar. Each year, a handful of mountaineers and hunters undertook the rigorous expedition which usually consisted of a 15 day journey on horseback in each direction, which led them through mountain passes exceeding an altitude of 12,000 feet; expeditions which were not only rich in sporting reminiscences but also left an unforgettable impression.

With independence in 1947 and the dispute between India and Pakistan over Kashmir, the curtain came down and foreigners, with rare exceptions, were forbidden entry into Ladakh. The Chinese-Indian conflict of 1962 accentuated the country's strategic importance and closed it yet more firmly to outsiders. All hopes to see it re-opened seemed destined to be put off indefinitely. At the time, the influx of large numbers of Indian soldiers constituted virtually the only "tourism". Remarkably, many of them quickly learned to appreciate those fascinating highlands, despite their climate which must have been particularly arduous for those accustomed to warmer climes. Some prolonged their stay, and, their term of military service finished, married Ladakhi girls and settled down permanently. Such cases were numerous in the Nubra Valley on the north side of the Ladakh chain, an area which has been described as most enchanting although, for reasons of security, as yet closed to foreign visitors.

In spite of its closure, Ladakh's reputation was not altogether lost among lovers of the Himalayas. Thus no great publicity was necessary to attract the country's first visitors when it was finally reopened. Their accounts of their experiences were sufficient to provoke a flood of tourists which has since rolled into Leh, the country's tiny capital, by land and by air. Indeed, the dimensions of this tourist deluge underline an undeniable fact: Ladakh has become "fashionable".

This new status is similarly reflected by a growing number of publications devoted to the land and people of Ladakh. The appearance of these works, though their quality may sometimes be dubious, can certainly be interpreted as demonstrating a sincere desire on the part of western travellers to better grasp the complexities of this extraordinary country.

Siddiq Wahid is in a unique position to contribute to such an understanding; he is Ladakhi and thus of Ladakhi mother tongue. In addition, he possesses all the necessary intellectual and academic equipment for communicating with a western public; his long and extensive studies of Tibetan culture at Harvard University in the United States culminated in a doctoral thesis on the well-known epic of Ling Kesar, still popular in Tibet and among other peoples of central Asia as well as in Ladakh, where many elderly villagers still know it by heart.

Mr. Wahid's remarks, contained in the following pages, are witness not only to a wealth of knowledge and comprehension of his subject, but also to a profound attachment born of many generations; he belongs to a Radhu family, established for two and a half centuries at Leh, and among the most eminent of the Muslim community.

The Sheikh Asad Radhu came to Ladakh from Srinagar to spread the teachings of Islam. His words must have reached many ears and touched many spirits, for an inscription in Persian testifies to his memory at the Sunni mosque at Leh which, at 10,000 feet, is perhaps the world's highest mosque. It is worth mentioning that this missionary activity did not seem at all to bother the Buddhist majority for Farok Radhu, son of the Sheikh of Ladakh, maintained close relations with the "gyalpo", or King of Ladakh, who offered him an estate at Stok, about 15 kilometres from Leh.

It was with Farok Radhu that the family's merchant vocation was established. His caravans followed the trails of Tibet as far as Lhasa, traversing the formidable mountain passes of Karakoram, and traded with Yarkand and other commercial centres of Chinese Turkestan. Although his descendants spread to these remote regions, the family maintained its center at Leh, which became one of the busiest commercial crossroads of Central Asia.

From that moment on, the Radhu family held an eminent and much-envied social position in Ladakh. In the small capital of Leh they owned numerous fine houses, the oldest of which was erected on the same rock as the royal palace. The family was widely known, their reputation

10

extending well beyond the city's confines. It should be noted that this eminent Muslim family has always maintained excellent relations with the Buddhist majority. Certain individual members made mixed marriages, creating family ties far more enduring than religious differences. An interesting illustration of the extraordinary integration of this Muslim family into the Ladakhi milieu was the Lopchak caravan. This was a semi-official, semi-commercial convoy which, by virtue of a treaty dating from the eighteenth century, travelled every other year from Leh to Lhasa delivering presents to the Dalai Lama and paying him respectful greetings on the part of the Ladakhi Buddhist community. Curiously, the Lopchak caravan remained during several generations a veritable monopoly of the Sheikh Radhu's descendants; it would thus appear that Ladakhi Buddhists had not the least objection to being represented before the highest authority of their religion by Muslims!

Khwaja Abdul Wahid Radhu, Siddiq Wahid's father, took part in the penultimate Lopchak expedition in 1942. He related his experience in a recent book entitled *Tibetan Caravan*, in which he also gives accounts of life in Ladakh at a time when one single mule track linked it with the outside world.

In a book called *Transhimalayas*, giving an account of his expeditions to Western Tibet, Sven Hedin often mentions the Radhus, though he does not refer to them by this name, as most of the family's members had ceased to carry it during the nineteenth century. Having been offered invaluable assistance by a great uncle of Siddiq Wahid, Ghulam Rasul, the Swedish explorer sought a reward for him from the Viceroy of India, Lord Minto. Ghulam Rasul thus received a certificate, still carefully preserved by his descendants, authorising him to add the title "Khan Bahadur" to his name.

Since that time, the trading caravans of Asia's highlands gradually declined in importance, disappearing altogether after the Communist rise to power in China and the subsequent occupation of Tibet. The borders were closed and Ladakh stifled. The Radhus were forced to "recycle" themselves and most abandoned Leh, which soon resembled no more than a sleepy village, to settle elsewhere, often in Kashmir.

By virtue of his intelligence and excellent academic results, Siddiq Wahid obtained a grant permitting him to study at one of the best regarded American universities. Eight years spent in the West did not, however, convert him to its ideas and mentality. On the contrary, his experiences in a world so fundamentally different from his own led him to reaffirm his convictions and identity as an oriental, faithful to his homeland and its traditional values. While assimilating a vast body of knowledge centered on Tibet and Tibetan culture, he progessively deepened his comprehension of the meaning of that culture, especially in light of what seemed to him the spiritual sterility of modern civilization. A religious man, he experienced a reinforcement of his own faith, Islam, and discovered its mystical dimension in Sufism. Through this, he gained a wider perspective which led to a renewed understanding of Buddhism, a religion which had long been tolerated and respected by his ancestors.

On his return to Ladakh he met Kenneth Storm, a talented photographer seeking new horizons. The young American, likewise a religious man, was not only struck by the majestic beauty of the Himalayas, but also by the feeling that they provided, thanks to their inhabitants' unfailing fidelity to their traditions, refuge for the sacred amidst a world transformed, and sometimes disfigured, by modernism. These two men, one a Muslim, the other a Christian, instinctively discovered a firm basis for friendship. In a space of three months, and with invaluable aid and guidance from his new friend, Storm had gathered an admirable collection of pictures.

Two talents naturally so complimentary could not fail to produce an illustrated work worthy of Ladakh. Only one problem arose: Kenneth Storm's photographs had been taken exclusively in summer. To depict this mountainous land without mention of winter, the season of its most important monastic festivities, would be to neglect one of its most spectacular and captivating aspects. It was decided that he would return to complete his task.

Upon his arrival in Ladakh, the photographer was received by Abdul Ghafoor, Siddiq's youngest brother, who was to be his new guide. A most unusual guide, however, for he was nearly blind, the victim of a merciless disease rendering even the most modern medical techniques impotent. This young man is progressively losing his sight and will soon be blind. At the beginning of 1980, he could still see well enough to avoid obstacles in his path. One of their joint excursions led them along the banks of the entirely frozen river Zangskar, with temperatures falling to between 20 and 30 degrees below zero. It was a dangerous expedition, but a fruitful one, thanks to the diligence of the young guide who, despite his handicap, acted as interpretor and diplomat, consistently establishing excellent relations with the local population.

He never uttered a word of complaint; on the contrary, his calm acceptance of his destiny exemplifies one of the fundamental virtues of Islam, or indeed, of any real religion. This attitude of serene resignation has as its foundation one inflexible condition: that he be permitted to remain in Ladakh. For he knows that the noise and movement of life in a big town such as Delhi or Srinagar would unsettle him and, especially at a moment when he consciously embraces a future in which he will become increasingly withdrawn, render him less sensitive to his innermost self. No environment could be more appropriate to such spiritual self-awareness than Ladakh, that magical place which, with regard to the outside world, might well be compared with what Muslims call a "khalwa", a spiritual retreat to a Himalayan summit.

Roger Du Pasquier

12

# THE PAST

It is a fashion these days, especially among uninformed tour operators, to describe Ladakh[1] as a land remote in both space and time. However, for one who wants to learn something of the land and its people, such a description greatly hinders an understanding of the civilization. The fact is that Ladakh is "remote" only for those who insist on regarding the country from Europe or the Americas. The land is towards the centre of the inner Asian[2] mass and has undoubtedly been the arena for many a cultural exchange over the years. Some of these exchanges date from about the first century of the Gregorian calendar, and there were certainly even earlier contacts about which we know little. What historical sources we do have insist that for a full understanding of Ladakh's past, we should dip into our historical knowledge of Buddhist Central Tibet[3] and Islamic Middle East, of Mughal India and Turkish Kashgar, of Dogra Kashmir and Sikh Punjab, and, of course, British India. It is true that the extent of Ladakh's relationship with these cultures varies, but this vast inter-relationship of Ladakh with its neighbours and distant powers in itself is enough to dispel any rumours of "an isolated Ladakh".

Yet it is unfair to say that the notion that Ladakh is remote is without any basis. The isolation of Ladakh has its origins in the mid-nineteenth century. All during the eighteenth to the late nineteenth centuries it was British policy to prevent covetous eyes being cast on her interests in Asia. To protect them she sought to form a "buffer zone" from as far west as Afghanistan right across the Transhimalaya. Ladakh formed part of this strategy, which was directed primarily against Russia. To operate this strategy, the British Indian authorities preferred to work through the Dogra regime of Jammu and Kashmir, with whom the Crown's representatives had a special relationship, rather than deal directly with the Ladakhis. Therefore, so as not to offend their Dogra allies, the British were selective regarding the travel of Europeans in Ladakh, making the latter region inaccessible to the average westerner. However, it is as well to remember that that was a recent phenomenon and an artificial, political barrier.

Another tendency is to think of Ladakh as an "exotic" land. This is an intellectual simplification that Ladakhis find, at the very least, patronising. A *simplification*, because most of the world's population lives as the Ladakhi does and not as the westerner in modern times. In other words, the Ladakhi earns his livelihood by means which do not allow for the pursuit of extraordinary leisure or for a large surplus in commodities. Instead he pursues his profession

– be it farmer, metal-worker, weaver or carpenter – as a traditional artisan who works in concord with nature and, on a higher level, seeks to "imitate nature in her way of operation". These are the qualities which permit the Ladakhi, for instance, to chant the sacred formula *Om mani padme hum* to the rhythm of almost any activity. Any particular physical labour is thereby consecrated, given spiritual meaning. It is this that the Ladakhi has in common with most of Asia and Africa.

Therefore Ladakh is not "exotic" simply because her way of life is lost to those who hold a monopoly of world economy or mass communication. It is a living, breathing culture. To study its history or portray it as a cultural museum-piece is a gross injustice to its inhabitants and its traditions. For we ought to regard the Ladakhi's meaningful existence centered around work, prayer and contemplation, not as an antiquated relic, but rather as a lesson in and a reminder of a valuable way of life for all mankind.

This should be borne in mind in order to understand the portrait of Ladakh presented here.


# The Mon, the Dard and Early Tibetan Influences

The history of Ladakh prior to the seventh century is obscure. This is partly because the period has not received the attention of scholars, and partly because written documents concerning it are scarce. It has been suggested that certain places mentioned in the accounts of ancient chroniclers such as Herodotus and Ptolemy correspond to areas in Ladakh. Indeed at least two such identifications, that of the Balti and the Dard, are generally accepted as correct. But these researches, the conclusions of which are based on philological reasoning, are far from giving us a complete picture. It is to be hoped that the recent upsurge of interest in the language, history and general anthropology of the Himalayas will someday help to shed more light on the ancient history of Ladakh.

This does not mean, however, that we need be totally in the dark regarding ancient Ladakh. Over the years the intellectual framework of the inhabitants of Ladakh, and the resulting material culture, have changed little. An unbiased, objective understanding of this can be revealing. In addition, in parts of the region it is possible to find traces of Ladakh which are hidden from the chronological point of view. These are the Mon and the Dard, both of whom were the early inhabitants of the area. A close look at the lives of these people will give us more information about ancient Ladakh.

The term Mon is found across the Himalaya and is generally applied to valley-dwellers by the Tibetan-speaking peoples. The Ladakhi Mon people appear, at some point, to have been important members of society, if not the rulers of the land. It was during this time that the Mon constructed, or were at least the patrons of the artisans who constructed, many of the castles that are found in various parts of Ladakh, most notably in Zangskar. The Mon have been Buddhists since the time of Kaniska and were probably instrumental in the importing of motifs in Tibetan art which are based directly on the Indian tradition. That is, without Chinese or Tantric influences. An agricultural community, the Mon are fond of music and in the Ladakh of today they remain as official musicians of villages, providing the latter with music on festive occasions. In the winter months, when work in the fields comes to a standstill, some of them also chant the traditional epic of the Tibetan speaking people – the *Ling Kesar*. Incidentally, this epic, which is chanted by non-Mon as well, holds many a key to the ways of life prior to Tibetan Buddhist influences.

Like the Mon, the Dard are an agricultural people. It is reasonable to assume that their influx into Ladakh was not achieved without some fighting, as their interests – fieldwork – were identical to those of the Mon. The Dard are an Indo-European people who inhabit the region where the Hindukush, the Himalayas and the Pamirs face each other. These people migrated to Ladakh at an early date – it is not as yet possible to fix an exact time – and settled in the Dras valley, Da and Hanu. The Dards of Dras converted to Islam some 300 years ago and retain little of their ancient religious customs. Those of Da-Hanu, however, to this day manifest their pre-Buddhist customs and, perhaps, beliefs; although they are nominally Buddhists. Indeed, a leading investigator of Dard beliefs and culture, Professor Karl Jettmar, feels that the ancient religion of the Dardic people is the best preserved in the Da-Hanu area[4].

In the seventh and eighth centuries, a degree of Tibetanisation took place in Ladakh. This is shown by the fact that Chinese chronicles of those years refer to the areas east of Baltistan as Tibet; and Ladakh is what exists "east of Baltistan". In fact, it is quite possible that the inhabitants of Ladakh felt Tibetan influence even earlier, for the nomadic Tibetans of the Chang-thang would have had good reason to have contacts with the sedentary Mon and Dard, exchanging grain for animal products. At any rate, by the mid-seventh century, during the reign of King Songstan Gampo of Central Tibet, Ladakh became increasingly aware of her eastern neighbour. During that period, the Tibetan nomads of the Chang-thang probably inter-married with the Mon-Dard population and allowed a trading or bartering system to develop between the two groups of people.

This early Tibetanisation was in all likelihood complemented by influence from Kashmir in the south-west. It has also been suggested that Ladakh was a principality under the political dominion of Lalitaditya-Muktapida (ca. AD 725–765), then the King of Kashmir[5]. But direct evidence for this is wanting. That Kashmir did exercise an influence on Ladakh at the

15

time is unquestionable, and is particularly visible in the field of art and architecture. Kashmiri Buddhist bronze statues are to be found in the various monasteries and an eighth century influence continued to show up through the years in stylized wood carvings at the early monasteries at Lamayuru, Basgo, Alchi and other places.

From the end of the ninth century, Central Tibetan culture began to make rapid gains in Ladakh. Thus, in order to understand the history of Ladakh at this juncture it is necessary to briefly recall the early history of Tibet. From the early seventh century to the mid-ninth century, Central Tibet steadily emerged as a military power in the Inner Asian region. While the aristocracy of the Yarlung Dynasty, the ruling dynasty of this period, was attempting to halt the erosion of its powers in the face of an expanding Buddhist clergy, the internal disunity does not appear to have affected Tibetan military prowess. The first united Tibet was strong enough to challenge the troubled T'ang Dynasty of China and even place a "puppet Emperor" on the throne at Chang-an in AD 768. It gained territories as far west as Wakhan and at times the Tibetans allied themselves to the expanding Arab kingdom to the west. It was not until the great Abbasid Caliph, Harun al-Rashid (AD 786–809) had reversed this policy and allied himself with the Chinese that the Tibetans suffered defeat.

Nevertheless, in spite of this activity on her borders, by the mid-ninth century the latent friction between the followers of Bon-Shamanism and Buddhism in Tibet began to rise in open rebellion. The King at this time was Ralpacan, a convinced Buddhist. He initiated many reforms such as special taxes to support clerical institutions. Such changes were resented and the dissent climaxed in the assassination of the King in AD 836. Ralpacan was succeeded by his elder brother, Lang Darma, who was anti-Buddhism. But by then the monarchy of a united Tibet had been dealt its death blow and concurrently Buddhism had gained a major foothold in the land. In the years to follow, the monarchy rapidly declined; Lang Darma himself was assassinated in AD 842 by a Buddhist monk, and Buddhism "went into hiding" in the border regions of Tibet. The monarchy was not to return to Central Tibet until a radical re-definition of its place and function had taken place. Buddhism re-emerged as a force in the mid-tenth century under the patronage of local hegemonies.

The line of the first Kings of Ladakh, known as the Lha Chen Dynasty, was descended from the infamous Lang Darma. Thus Ladakh was destined to be the inheritor and preserver of the monarchy of Tibet up to the mid-nineteenth century, although the actual powers of the monarchy were to fluctuate considerably during this period. Lang Darma had a son named Od Srungs by his younger queen. It was the grandson of this son, Skyid de Nyima Gon, who was forced to fly to western Tibet and subsequently consolidate his rule there. Upon his death, Nyima Gon's kingdom was divided between his

16

three sons, the eldest of whom, Lha Chen Pal gyi Gon, occupied the approximate area of present-day Ladakh. That is, the territory between the Zoji Pass and Rutog in the east. The rule of Nyima Gon's direct descendants continued until the fifteenth century.

Our information on the Lha Chen Dynasty is limited to a list of names, given in chronological order, which in itself is not without problems. However, these Kings set a pattern which continued to be followed through the years. Namely, the monarchy remained an institution for government which protected the state religion, Buddhism. And for a better understanding of the latter, Ladakh began to look increasingly towards Central Tibet. It was between the ninth and the mid-fifteenth centuries that the first texts on Tibetan Buddhism were copied in Ladakh. Most famous among those instrumental in this process is the outstanding scholar-monk Rinchen Zangpo, whose portrait is preserved on a mural composition at Alchi. The first Lamaseries were built during this period. Also, the tradition of sending novice monks to various monasteries in Central Tibet was initiated in the early fourteenth century and this served conclusively to Tibetanise Ladakh. Extensive as this Tibetanisation was, it must be pointed out that it did not go to the extent of mirroring the Tibetan system of governing; for in Ladakh the tasks of government were never placed directly in the hands of a religious head, as was the case in Tibet with the birth of the institution of the Dalai Lama's secular powers in the sixteenth century.

# The Namgyal Dynasty

Towards the end of the fifteenth century, the followers of Tsong Khapa (1357–1419), the famous commentator and synthesiser of Tibetan Buddhism, sent a mission to the western territories of the Tibetan cultural area. The Ladakhi King of that time received this mission favourably and established Spituk monastery on the banks of the Indus, the first monastery of the Gelugspa Order, later to be known as the Order of the Yellow Hats. Slowly other monasteries began to adhere to the rules of this new Order.

But unfortunately for the Gelugspa, the Lha Chen Dynasty was to come to an end and the succeeding Dynasty was to identify itself with the Ka gyud pa Order. A branch of the old Dynasty, which had its partisans in Tingmosgang, Basgo and other villages, emerged as a powerful rival. These descendants of the brother of the last Lha Chen King allied themselves to the people of Sheh village, and established a new dynasty which has been called the Namgyal Dynasty. Of this line of kings we know a little more.

The Namgyal Kings were to experience a series of military defeats as well as some victories, however short-lived these last may have been. They were to allow both Shi'i and Sunni Islam to make inroads into the culture. Tibetan influences were at their peak during the Namgyal period. Most of the palaces and citadels that are currently standing in Ladakh were built by them. And finally it was also the Namgyal Dynasty's fate to succumb to the methods and machinations of modern statecraft, with which they were unfamiliar, and be politically buried as a victim of the newly revised version of power politics. These policies were formulated, not by Ladakh's neighbours with whom she shared her borders, but in places as far away as London and Moscow.

The first Kings of the Namgyal Dynasty had to fend off the attempts of Mirza Haidar Dughlat, the general of the ruler of Kashgar in the north, to convert Ladakh to Islam. This was done successfully, but the Tibetan-speaking Balti people had submitted earlier. It was this Islamic influx which the rulers in Ladakh had to contend with during the final decades of the sixteenth century and later.

The various chieftains of the western Ladakhi territories were warring against each other, when Jamyang Namgyal (ca. 1575–1590) of Ladakh decided to enter the fray by backing one chieftain against another. Unluckily for him, he backed the wrong horse and found himself the prisoner of Ali Mir, the "Duke" of Puring. But fortune smiled because prison circumstances were relaxed enough to allow him to fall in love with his captor's daughter, Gyal Khatun, whom he married. The Ladakhi *on-po*, or astrologers, were afterwards inclined to recognize in the Muslim Gyal Khatun the reincarnation of the Buddhist female diety, White Tara. Thus, the likely inconveniences which may have arisen from this odd situation were resolved. While the marriage did not solve all future problems between Buddhist Ladakh and Muslim Baltistan, it was enough to ensure a period of relative tranquility for Ladakh's western frontier during the reign of King Sengge Namgyal, the descendant of Jamyang and his Balti wife.

Sengge Namgyal's military campaigns were directed primarily towards Guge in the east. In this conflict, he was victorious and it has earned him fame as the greatest King of Ladakh. Perhaps the title should be accorded him even more so because it was his reign that gave Ladakh many of the monuments that serve as reminders of Ladakh's glory for the following generations. He was a patron of the Tibetan monk Stag Tsang Ras Chen, and together they built the famous monastery of Hemis. Stakna and Chemre monasteries were also founded during his reign. So was the large old Palace at Leh which is now in ruins. To Stag Tsang Ras Chen is also attributed the introduction of the *mani ringmo*, or consecrated walls, which are a familiar landmark in Ladakh.

It was Sengge's grandson, Delegs Namgyal (ca. 1675–1705) who was to preside over the beginning of the dismemberment of the Ladakhi kingdom. This King, as ill-advisedly as his ancestor Jamyang Namgyal, interfered in a war which was being carried out hundreds of miles away from Ladakh's borders between Bhutan and Tibet. Delegs offered his services to the head

Lama of Bhutan where the order of Tibetan Buddhism that the Namgyal Dynasty favoured, the *Dukpa Ka Gyudpa,* was paramount. Tibet responded by attacking Ladakh with help from a Mongol army. Delegs in turn asked the ruler of Mughal Kashmir to help him, and the latter complied under the condition that the King embrace Islam, a mosque be built in Leh, and certain trade regulations be followed[6]. Once the Mughals successfully expelled the Mongol army and withdrew, however, the Tibetans returned behind the Mongol army and imposed their own conditions, among which were more trade regulations and the institution of a tribute, to be sent regularly to the Dalai Lama's government in Lhasa.

As if to recuperate from these devastating wars and treaties, the following years were spent in consolidating what was left of the kingdom and increasingly drawing closer to Central Tibet. In the early part of the eighteenth century the King started a system of appointing elders in villages to help him rule. These are probably the administrative antecedents of the *gopa*, or village headman, of today. A printing press to publish religious texts was also set up at that time. Towards the latter half of the century, primogeniture was formally introduced as a means for determining succession to the throne, as was the system of sending the younger brothers of the reigning King to various monasteries. Both these changes were introduced by Tibetan intervention. There was some internal unrest, as for instance when a certain King tried to impose more taxes than the normal, but the period in general was relatively calm. Islamic influences were also probably at their peak during this time, and we learn that King Tsetan Namgyal (died ca. 1790) was accomplished in Tibetan grammar and mathematics, and in Persian.

Although it was the Central Tibetans in the east and the Balti in the west who were the rivals with whom Ladakh was most familiar on the battlefield, it was not them but a third, unfamiliar, newly emerged power, the Dogra, which was to define Ladakh for the modern period.

The Dogra owed their rise to yet another people – the Sikh. The Sikhs were led by Maharajah Ranjit Singh, who had conquered Kashmir from his base in Lahore. Ranjit Singh appointed a Dogra, Gulab Singh, as his governor at Jammu. It was the military adventurer, Zorawar Singh, a general in the Jammu Governor's army, who pointed his sword towards Ladakh.

Already, before Zorawar Singh's invasion, the enigmatic Englishman, William Moorcroft[7], had travelled to Leh and, apparently without official sanction, tried to win over the King, Tsepal Namgyal, for British India. At that time the King had ignored Moorcroft. This he now tried to reverse, unsuccessfully, as the Dogra army marched through Ladakhi territories in Zangskar, Suru and up the Indus valley from Khalatse to the capital of Ladakh at Leh. Zorawar Singh had effectively conquered Ladakh. However, in the winter of 1841 he campaigned against Central Tibet. By undertaking this, Zorawar made the Napoleonic error of challenging a people who had lived through many a difficult winter in their own territory and, more importantly, he moved against them in their worst season. The Dogra army was defeated and Zorawar himself killed.

Meanwhile in the Punjab, Anglo-Sikh relations were not at their best. In 1846 the Sikhs were defeated in a war against the British. Significantly for Ladakh, Gulab Singh failed to aid his Sikh patrons in Lahore, for which he was rewarded by the British with the newly created State of Jammu and Kashmir. Ladakh was included in this State and since that time the position of the Ladakhi ruler is best described as that of a vassal king under the Maharajah of Kashmir. For the administration of Ladakh and Baltistan, the Maharajah appointed a *Wazir*, while to supervise trade with Central Asia the British posted a Joint Commissioner, both of whom were to share political authority in Ladakh.

This state of affairs existed for the remaining hundred years of the British Raj. In 1947, when the sub-continent became independent, the then Maharajah of Kashmir, Hari Singh, was given the option of ceding to India or Pakistan. Waiting literally until the last moment, the Maharajah opted for India. Thus Ladakh's political future became linked to India's.

# Footnotes to The Past

[1] LADAKH is the Anglicised spelling of the name which is pronounced La-dags by the inhabitants of the region. Early British explorers wrote LADAK, which too is incorrect. But later they adopted the current spelling of the word. The spelling LADAKH probably came into use after the Islamic incursions into the area. The word was written or pronounced with the final "k" changed to the guttural "kh" of the Arabic script when used in Urdu or Persian.

A word regarding the transliteration of Tibetan words into the Roman script is perhaps in order here. As this book is not meant exclusively for the specialist, we have written Ladakhi words with a view to facilitating correct pronounciation. A large number of Tibetan words consist of consonant clusters and the rules of grammar are such that these are either ignored or create sounds of an entirely different character. All this, we felt, would only serve to confuse the reader unfamiliar with literary Tibetan.

[2] The term "Inner Asia" is being used more and more to define the land mass from the Altai mountains in the north-east in China to the Urals in the west, and from the Afghan Pamirs and the northern slopes of the Himalayas to the Siberian Plains. It is used in this text with the above definition in mind.

[3] A word needs to be said about the use of certain terms. CENTRAL TIBET and LADAKH are political designations to be understood according to their current boundaries. By contrast TIBETAN-SPEAKING AREAS OR PEOPLES is a linguistic and cultural designation meant to include both Ladakh and Central Tibet, but also other areas influenced by Tibetan culture. These are Bhutan Sikkim, parts of Nepal, Lahoul, Spiti and Baltistan. Thus it makes sense to talk of "Tibetan" when speaking of the language of Ladakh.

[4] Cf. Dr Karl Jettmar, "Ethnological Research in Dardistan 1958" in PROCEEDINGS OF THE AMERICAN PHILOSOPHICAL SOCIETY, Vol. 105, No. 1, 1961.

[5] Cf. Snellgrove and Skrupski, THE CULTURAL HERITAGE OF LADAKH, Prajna Press, Boulder.

[6] The first of these conditions had only a nominal effect. The second condition had a more substantial effect in that a mosque was built in Leh, which in turn served to nurture a rather sizeable Sunni Muslim population in the region.

[7] There are many legends about Moorcroft. A very able summary of his adventures (and, incidentally, a well-balanced introduction to the region as well) are to be found in John Keay's two books, WHEN MEN AND MOUNTAINS MEET and THE GILGIT GAME.

*The skull and horns of a urial, a wild sheep found in Ladakh, keep a ghostly watch over the mountain track.*

*Following double page: Fotaksar village hangs on the edge of seamed and gullied silt cliffs, which were deposited by a now vanished lake.*

*Winter can sometimes improve communications in Ladakh, for frozen rivers provide a highway. By using the Zangskar river, Ladakhis can cover the journey from Spadum to Leh in five to seven days, instead of the ten to fifteen needed for the high route used in summer when the gorge is a raging mountain torrent. A party of Ladakhis moves in single file up the Zangskar Gorge below Chiling.*

*Ladakh geology: the twisted strata give an idea of the tremendous pressures that thrust up the mountains.*

*Tracks in the snow diverge to pass on either side a group of Ch'ortens and mani ringmo, or consecrated walls, near Thikse monastery. Travellers must always keep these monuments on their right.*

*A driving snowstorm casts a wintery veil over the landscape as a man leads his dzo, a cross between a yak and cow, homeward.*

# THE PRESENT

In the tale about the great hero of the Tibetan-speaking peoples, Gyapo Kesar, there is a passage in which the invention of the modern gun is narrated in a very interesting manner. It is explained that prior to the gun, the mode of hunting was the bow and arrow. Now the gods saw the destruction being wrought by this weapon and in turn revealed the gun. The benefit of this new weapon, it is explained, was that it made a loud bang when used, thereby warning the other animals of the hunter's presence and saving further damage!

In the tradition of story-telling, this passage is a unique example of how new ideas are blended into an ancient saga without destroying the values that are an integral part of the original story. It is an example of versatility in the art of adapting to change, which is in the nature of this world, without succumbing to change as an absolute value in itself. To those who have visited Ladakh in the past five years, it will be evident as to why the above story is quoted. Present-day Ladakh will have to gather all its resources in the art of healthy adaptibility if its culture is not going to suffer a psychological rupture which will in effect destroy it.

It is true that the forces of modernisation which have been unleashed upon Ladakh seem to be overwhelming. The often uncritical adoption of modern attitudes presents an added threat to the sanity of the land. While many enlightened Ladakhis, aware of the excesses of the modern age, are sincerely troubled by the present, pessimism is an underestimation of the facts and can often lead to resignation and a lack of action, which is what Ladakh needs least at this time.

The fact is that Ladakh has not undergone any severe or radical change as of today. The people still live very much as they did over the past centuries. If not forced, Ladakh need not be dependent on modern systems of social relations, economy, and technology. It cannot remain isolated, it is true, but this state of affairs (of doubtful value) should not be used as an excuse to allow the dismantling of an entire infrastructure of social and spiritual attitudes towards life. Rather, it should be realized that the formal aspects of modernisation can be accepted as being in the nature of things, as one aspect of the *kali yuga*[1]; at the same time it needs to be recognised that it is not necessary to accept the *consequences* of modernisation, consequences which are apparent in the mechanical rejection of traditional social values, in the breakdown of family relationships and ultimately in the casual abandoning of *dharma*, that is, religion.

29

*Typical of the mountain scenery in Ladakh, blue waters from distant glaciers tumble down the rocky Valley of Hanupata.*

It has just been stated that Ladakh has not experienced great changes as of yet. This may be puzzling to people not entirely familiar with Ladakh. The bazaars in Leh, Kargil and one or two more central towns in Ladakh provide the population with most of the objects of modern invention and show evidence of great changes. However, this ostensible "progress" is limited to those towns and the influx of villagers who come to visit them occasionally. By and large, the villages are still unaffected. Life in them will be described in the following pages, giving an idea of how the majority of Ladakhis live today.

## Community Life

The average Ladakhi family consists of husband, wife and their children. Unlike other parts of India, there is not the common notion of the extended family, where the grandparents live under the same roof. As soon as a son, or in some cases a son-in-law, is capable of fending for himself the parents move out of the original house into a smaller house called the *khang-bu*. The "independence" of the son is determined by his ability, with the help of his wife, to till the land and sufficiently provide for the children and themselves. Thus, the grandparents are often found living with the family until the grandchildren are old enough to either help in the fields or look after the younger children. Once they move into a *khang-bu*, the grandparents are provided with a piece of land which they till for their own needs until they die.

There are, however, exceptions to this rule of the grandparents moving out of the family house. It is less the case among richer people and the practice is looked down upon by some Muslim Ladakhis. Here the more conventional notion of the extended family can be found.

Several travellers have commented on the constant activity of the people of Ladakh. One of the first Europeans to come to Ladakh, Father Ippolito Desideri, was commenting on the people of the Central Tibetan plateau when he noted his impressions, but they may be said to be true of Ladakh also. "By nature the Thibettans are seldom idle or lazy but generally occupied with something. Indeed one may say they are more or less skilled in all things necessary for everyday life."[2]

As might be imagined, Ladakhis move to the rhythm of nature. Late spring and summer is the time for tilling the land and tending the cattle. Autumn gives a pause long enough to collect fuel for the winter months and mend or make winter apparel. The winter months are spent in making household items such as carpets, ropes and baskets. Early spring initiates the cycle once again as farmers prepare the fields for crops by spreading manure and reinforcing the top soil for the planting season.

The mountains dominate more than just the landscape of Ladakh. As the winter months draw to a close Ladakhi farmers anxiously look to the peaks to see how much snow remains on them. Lucky is the village which has a towering mountain behind it, for it means that much more water from the melting snows. When May approaches, the ground is sufficiently soft to allow it to be ploughed. In mid June the sun is strong enough to melt the snow on the glaciers and a steady stream begins to flow down the numerous gorges. These are channeled into the village's many fields by the village *chu-pon*, literally, "Lord of the water", the person responsible for the fair distribution of the irrigation waters.

The village itself is divided into several sections, called *chu-tso*, or "village section". Each section has a representative whose task it is to assure the smooth running of his area. The village as a whole elects, usually for a period of three years, a person known as the *go-pa*, or headman, who, along with the officials already mentioned and others, administers the village. Recently a parallel administrative system has been set up by the Government. As would be expected, some tensions do arise from this duplication, but it is as yet too early to fully assess the effects of the new situation.

The villager buys from the nearest town such items as tea, sugar, rice and spices. In the past few years the practice of buying utensils and, perhaps, clothing, has gained some popularity. Basically, however, the village still relies on its own resources for much of its needs. When far from a town this holds even truer.

There is also the traditional bartering, which is still carried on. Thus, a person who has a large supply of willow may exchange it for grain, or even one type of grain can be exchanged for another. The cereals that are grown are mainly barley and wheat. As a rule barley is planted in the villages that are higher up and wheat, which requires more sun, is planted in the villages at lower altitudes. After the harvest, if a family has only one or the other, these commodities are bartered, usually in equal proportions.

Similarly there is a system for bartering labour. Since all planting or cutting is not done at the same time, there being a few days' difference in when individual families undertake these tasks, each family has an arrangement by which it shares its labour with another family. The method for doing this is quite well established; so much so that there are different terms, for instance, when labour is bartered for the sowing season and when it is bartered for the harvest season.

Each community is self-sufficient in having skilled craftsmen as well. Perhaps the largest number of skilled craftsmen in any village are the masons. But there are also carpenters, blacksmiths, metal workers, wood carvers and painters. It is the skill of these artisans that determines the artistic quality of a village. Often a well-to-do individual will call a particularly good craftsman from a neighbouring village to work for him. Some craftsmen, like those of the village of Chiling, are known all over Ladakh for their metal-working skills.

In between the sowing and the harvesting seasons, during July and August, villagers can be seen trudging up the valleys driving their cattle before them. Their destination is the village *phu*, or high country, where they are taking their cattle to graze. It is seen as a time for picnicing and relaxing. But here too there is work to be done. The dung of the *dzo* and cows must be collected for winter fuel, milk must be churned to extract butter and make *tara*, a semi-fermented drink. These are then bottled and canned to be taken home. The villagers stay at the *phu* for anywhere from fifteen days to a month, at which time they once again pack up their belongings, load their mules, *dzo* or horses and head back down to the village. Some of them will return to the *phu*, if they can harvest early enough, to collect more fuel and save on fodder by grazing their cattle for a few extra days in the highlands.

The first item to be harvested is the tall grass called *ol*. It is planted as fodder for the animals and stored for the winter. The barley and wheat follow.

Once the harvesting is completed and the family has returned, perhaps from its second trip to the *phu*, the field work is essentially done. All the animals are released, so that they may graze on the stubble of the harvested crops, after which the land is ploughed for a second time. This in order to ensure that the first waters that fall on the terraced slopes do not simply run off the fields.

As they settle in for the winter months, Ladakhis may be heard to say, "Ah! Winter has arrived. There is no more work." What is meant is that there is no more field work. Field work requires both men and women to get up before dawn to ensure proper irrigation, to cut the wheat and barley while sitting on their haunches for hours at a time and to carry huge sacks of cut and threshed grain to the watermills lined along the village's main stream for grinding. This work finishes in the winter until the next summer. But also gone are the occasions when it was possible to sit outdoors after a hard day's work and comfortably sip *chang*, the mildly intoxicating brew extracted from the lowest quality barley and brewed in individual homes.

With the coming of winter a monastic calm pervades the land. The number of cloudy days increases and movement outside the home is restricted to essential purposes like feeding and watering the animals. If the village is near Leh or some other large town, one member of the household may have to venture out on a regular basis to go to his office desk. For the others it is time to busy themselves with indoor tasks. Out come the raw wool collected from the goats, the spindle, the loom, needle and thread. As one member of the family cleans the wool, another spins thread on the spindle. Others huddle around the open fire in the kitchen and deftly use needle and thread to complete a shoe or mend a torn *gos*, the long gown worn by the Ladakhi. A limited number of families may have the good fortune to possess a member who can work the loom and weave a carpet.

32

*The summer route from Spadam to Leh forms a striking contrast with the frozen river track shown on page 25. The track leads through a rocky defile. Thomson, the traveller, writing in 1848 remarked that the sun could not possibly reach the bottom of the dark shady dell.*

*Following double page:*
*Donkeys laden with fodder are guided across one of the flat, lonely plains of Ladakh.*

*A primitive bridge, woven of willow twigs, sags dangerously close to the swollen waters of the Zangskar, near Pidmo.*

*A young boy crosses a pass, keeping the* mani ringmo, *consecrated wall, and the prayer flag on his right, as custom dictates.*

*Following double page: Prayer flags flutter from Namgyal Peak, above Leh, and add a splash of colour to the sombre grey of the cloudy winter landscape.*

*A thin layer of powdery snow dusts the tents set up to form a make-shift bazaar for visitors to the Thikse monastery festival.*

*A Ladakhi village house, showing fodder being spread out to dry on the flat roof.*

*Thikse monastery. At the end of a festival, villagers file home, as always keeping the Ch'orten to their right.*

Talismans to ward off earth-demons are found outside all Ladakhi houses. A ram's skull, with the horns pointing downwards to the earth is surrounded by an elaborate array of strings and other mystic objects.

*Ladakhis in procession pass a group of Ch'ortens below the monastery of Likir. Ch'ortens, which vary in size and type, are perhaps the most conspicuous religious symbols in Ladakh. The name means literally "receptacle for offerings". Most Ch'ortens are erected in memory of Buddha or of saints. They represent the five elements into which man's body is resolved after death. The solid rectangular base represents the solidity of the Earth; the globe above, Water; the triangular spire, Fire; the crescent, like the inverted vault of the sky, Air; while the circle, tapering in flame into space, represents the Ether.*

44

Winter begins in November and the cold lasts for about five months. Life during this time is centered around the elegant mud-brick house. Most Ladakhi houses are flat-roofed with a court yard in the middle. After entering the main door of the house, the stable where the animals are kept is first encountered. It forms part of the ground floor. The animals kept here usually consist of *dzo*, cows, mules, goats and sheep. A well-to-do household may own a yak and horses as well.

Climbing a flight of steps, the visitor passes through a hallway leading to an upper courtyard. Here are the rooms where the family lives. The largest room, and most occupied in winter, is the kitchen. Along one wall runs a set of shelves where the gleaming brass and copper utensils are proudly displayed. In the centre of the room is a small pit where, during winter mornings and evenings, a fire is lit to warm all hands. Below the kitchen is the "wine cellar" where the *chang* is prepared and stored.

The roof of the house is flat with a parapet, anywhere from a few inches to a foot and a half high, running along its edges. Close to the parapet is kept the fodder for the animals, for the roof is a convenient storage area, as it allows the fodder to dry further in the dry air. Some houses have a small room at one corner called the *shel-khang*, or glass room. It is so called because the room has one or two sides made with glass panes. These sides face south and east, allowing a maximum of the sun's rays to warm it up and, understandably, this makes it a favourite room in the winter.

If the winter months were an entirely indoor affair, it would indeed be boring. But it is the season when almost all the monasteries celebrate their individual festivals. People count the days from one festival to another and much of the time is taken up in planning to travel to each of these celebrations. Methods of travel are a little easier now, as the buses which ply between villages abandon their regular schedules during the festival days to help transport as many people as possible to the monasteries. On the morning of a particular festival large groups of villagers dressed in their best can be seen anxiously looking for vehicles at the village bus stop. As a bus or jeep approaches the stop, the people rush on to it and, having found a seat, wait for it to take them to their destination.

More than for the general public, the monastery, or *gompa*, festivals are an occasion for the monks, or *taba*[3], to assume openly their position in society. As the first rays of the sun hit the mountains, monks blow the large copper trumpets from the roof-top of their monastery. Meanwhile, down below in the courtyard, feverish preparations begin. The various ritual articles are laid out, and within the main assembly hall monks put on the vestments and masks, ready for the dances which are the chief attraction. The first big event of the day is the unfurling of the large *thanka*, or painted scroll. As events build up to this the music gets louder, incense is brought out and a group of monks in ceremonial dress comes out and witnesses the display of the *thanka*.

In the meantime people are streaming in from the villages. The festival is a time when the monastery abandons its privacy as the laity freely roams about paying homage in the various chapels. It is as if a mutual exchange takes place between the monks and the laity, the former allowing the outside world to invade them and the latter experiencing a striking measure of the spiritual life. Offerings of butter, oil, incense and money are placed before the deities with the assistance of attendant lamas. Outside the walls of the monastery merchants are setting up tents displaying wares such as dried apricots, sweets, gaily coloured scarves, oil, butter and incense. Some set up chairs and tables for a make shift restaurant or even games of chance.

The entrance of the Head Lama, the *Rinpoche*, is perhaps the most spectacular event of the entire festival. During the year he is not very visible. He is either engrossed in his studies or meditation, and when he does walk around the monastery it is not easy to distinguish him from the other inhabitants. But the festival is a time for him to assume his rôle as Master. To the accompaniment of ritual music and chants he enters the courtyard and seats himself on his throne to witness the ceremonies.

As the masked dancers whirl about, jumping into the crowds and distributing sweets, it is possible to think of the ceremonies solely as "entertainment". In fact these festivals are solemn occasions where, among other things, a thanksgiving is offered for the arrival of the solstice and prayers directed against disease, famine and other calamities.[4]

Indeed, even the events which are "pure entertainment" take place with the blessings of the lama. One such happening is the archery contest in the summer months. Each section of a village has its own contests for which only the families living in that particular section are invited. The shooting is at a target and the matches usually last for two or three days. When someone hits the bull's eye there are loud exclamations and the person is garlanded with a *kha-dags*, the ceremonial white cotton or silk scarf which is common to all Tibetan-speaking areas.

When the archers stop for a while, the floor is occupied by dancers composed of men and women from the village. Ladakhi dancing involves movements primarily of the hands and the feet, the latter shuffling to the rhythmic beating of the drum played by the village's Mon family or two, the musicians of Ladakh. The sun's setting is the signal to bring out the *chang* which is drunk freely on such days. The music and dancing go on far into the night giving the young men and women of the village a chance to meet each other and, perhaps, discreetly choose a future mate, thereby setting the stage for an "arranged marriage".

As in any traditional society, important events in life are determined in consultation with priest, parents and family members. A marriage is more commonly initiated by the male side. The parents, usually when their son is twenty years old, go to the house of the intended bride with an offer of *chang*

46

and formally ask for the hand of the girl, who is probably two to three years younger than the boy. If the match is agreed upon, lamas are consulted and a day for the ceremony fixed.

Almost the entire expense of the marriage feast is borne by the villagers, who come once they are informed of the match. Each family attending the wedding brings something for the feast; barley, wheat, sugar, dried apricots, butter, tea and milk are among the usual gifts. The host family keeps careful note of what is brought so that as each of his guests celebrates a similar event, they can return the gift they have received in proper proportion. The bride and the groom are offered *kha-dags* or ceremonial scarves, by guests, and sometimes a gift of money. While the bride is expected to sit through the day, the groom often joins in the dancing and, of course, drinking *chang*.

The marriage ceremony described above holds true largely for both Buddhist and Muslim Ladakhi weddings. There are some differences in that while in the Buddhist instance both men and women guests sit together, they are separated in the case of Muslims. Also, *chang* is not served at a Muslim wedding, Tibetan tea being the standard drink. While the rule is that the bride is brought to her husband's house, at times the husband may take up residence in the house of his in-laws. This is done in the event of the in-laws having no sons or when they are the wealthier family.

There is also a wedding which in Ladakhi is termed *skus te khyong ches*, literally "to bring by theft". Here the bride is the "stolen" individual. Some anthropologists are studying this phenomenon and believe that in ancient times there was a literal stealing of the bride. These days, however, the term signifies a wedding which is held without announcement and fanfare. While the method of arranging the marriage is similar, the bride is brought to her new home quietly. After a few days some relatives and close friends are invited for a meal and the general public is considered informed of the new relationship. Usually poorer families and individuals who are marrying for a second or third time, due to a divorce or a death, employ this method.

The birth of a child to the new couple is again an opportunity for the community to draw together and help out a needy family. For days, friends and relatives visit the household carrying gifts of food for the mother, usually *mar-zan*, a gruel made with butter and rice. At the same time, the lama is called to pray that the child may be protected from any untoward illness.

These days many villages have a primary school, and a larger village may even have a secondary school. Children are sent to attend these more and more. Even though he goes to school, the child is still, when old enough, called upon to help in the fields. It is quite usual, therefore, to have a high rate of absence for an older child during the harvest season. Yet parents generally take the education of their children seriously. When the opportunity presents itself they will often send their child for additional tuition during the winter months when the schools close. One of the reasons for this is that the ability to read and write is equated with gaining religious knowledge. Indeed the term used for these skills is *chos*, the Tibetan word meaning religion.

It has been mentioned already that when a child is old enough to help in the fields, it is time for the grandparents to move to a cottage house and cultivate a small piece of the family land for themselves. In this way the older generation continues to fend for itself until death.[5]

# The Religions

It is now apparent that religion is the backbone of all life in Ladakh. It punctuates the days, the months and the years of daily life. The more important rituals are performed by the monks, and often a household will invite a son or a brother who has gone to the village monastery to study and become a lama, to perform such duties. But the layman attends to rituals that he is in a position to perform, such as the lighting of the oil lamps before the family altar in the mornings, reading the scriptures and, of course, the continual chanting of the sacred formula, or *mantra, "om mani padme hum."*

While Buddhism is clearly the dominant religion of the region – this is true both from the physical perspective, the monuments to this tradition being the most numerous, as well as from the standpoint of population – it should be pointed out that other religions have also been represented in Ladakh for many years. These are Islam and Christianity. In this portion of the book we shall briefly discuss all these religions in their Ladakhi setting.

Tibetan Buddhism, the version found in Ladakh, is a many faceted tradition which has only recently begun to be studied and understood by non-practitioners. It should be remembered that it grew out of Indian Buddhism, and has maintained that link, for Tibetan Buddhism adheres strictly to the teachings of Siddhartha Gautama, universally known as the Buddha, or "Enlightened One". Therefore, to estrange Tibetan Buddhism from the teachings of its Founder in India, would be to deprive it of its foundations.

Siddhartha Gautama also gained fame as Shakyamuni, the Sage of the Shakyas, Shakya being the tribe to which he belonged. The Buddha lived and taught in a small principality at the foot of the Himalayas in the sixth century BC.

As with any other person who has similarly expounded profound religious truths, a vast corpus of literature has grown around the Buddha. Some of it is historical fact, some of it is legend.[6] Based on the latter category is a story about the young Gautama who, at certain points in his life saw successively an old man, a sick man, a funeral and a hermit. These phenomena led him to meditate on the existence of aging, sickness, death and contemplation. The first three of these phenomena he understood to be

48

*A Ladakhi woman, carrying a load of hay on her back, stops to look at the Leh bazaar. All year round, Ladakhis gather at Leh to barter or sell goods such as vegetables, fruit, grass, hay, and dung and wood for fuel.*

Daily life in Ladakh. Left: A Ladakhi plods towards the local butcher bent under a load of sheepskins. Above: Two Ladakhis using a pit saw to cut up a tree into material for building a new house. Below: Villagers drawing water from the well in winter when all the streams are frozen up. Right: Ladakhi women preparing the fields for the spring sowing.

Village life. Left: A Ladakhi weaving on a hand-made loom. Above: Family members of the Tascan House in Stok breakfast on nampe and buttered tea. Right: a butcher chops up fresh mutton on his block. Below: The Yogkma household in Chiling, the metal-working village. Morning activity centres around the stove as the sun slants through a thick haze of smoke.

Chiling is the centre for Ladakh's metalworking industry. The village, which consists of five houses, and four families, was first settled by a metal-worker imported from Nepal at the beginning of the seventeenth century. The descendants of this craftsman continue to follow his calling today. Far left: Craftsman Tsetan Angbo. Below left: Copper links for a tea kettle chain being prepared for firing. Centre: Namgyal Tsering hammering a spout for a tea-kettle. Today, steel anvils have replaced stones, and the brass and copper used at Chiling now come from India via the bazaar at Leh. Gold is seldom used nowadays. Below: Phuntzok Spalzang, at more than 72 the oldest Chiling master-craftsman. Left: An example of his skill: silverwork decorating the spout of a tea kettle.

indications of the impermanence of life on earth. The last he knew to be a Path which would lead to deliverance from the impermanent. Thus, he formulated the Four Noble Truths which are the very basis of the Buddhist canons. These are that suffering is in the nature of earthly existence, that this has a cause, that suffering must be destroyed and that there is a Path which enables this .

When the Buddha left this world his teachings were handed down from generation to generation of his followers and eventually committed to writing. Various facets of the teachings began to take shape and these were termed Nikaya Buddhism, Mahayana Buddhism and Tantric Buddhism. Mahayana Buddhism flourished during the seventh and eighth centuries and it was in this form that the religion first spread to Central Tibet. Buddhism was probably introduced in Ladakh at an earlier period, but it was in its Tibetan form that the religion came to stay until the present day. This occurred during the eleventh and the following centuries.

Once established in Tibet, more sects and interpretations of Buddhism followed. In the beginning there were sacred texts that needed to be translated from the Sanskrit originals. The Tibetan King, Songs-stan Gampo, established this practice by inviting various monks and scholars to do this for his subjects. In time Indian Masters came to Tibet and taught the people. One such was Padmasambhava in the mid-eighth century. The followers of this Master were called the *Nying-ma pa*, "the ancient ones". In the eleventh century, there lived a Tibetan Teacher named Milarepa. He came to be regarded as one of the most profound teachers and the line of teachings carried down from him and his Masters are known as the *Ka-gyud pa* teachings.[7] Towards the latter half of the fourteenth century there arose in Tibet a reforming school whose followers were called the *Gelugs pa*, or the "virtuous ones". The first Monk of this school was a man named Tsong-kha pa. The *Gelugs-pa* are also known as the "Yellow Hat Sect" and it is to this school that the Dalai Lama belongs.

In Ladakh it was a sub-order of the *Ka-gyud pa*, called the *Duk-pa*, and the *Gelugs-pa* order, that gained prominence. Most of the monasteries in the region subscribe to either one or the other of these two schools. Perhaps the best known monastery in Ladakh, Hemis, belongs to the *Duk-pa* order and it has several monasteries under its patronage. To the *Gelugs-pa* order belong such monasteries as Thikse, Spituk and Likir. Alchi, another monastery that has gained prominence following the researches of Professor David Snellgrove and Dr Tadeuz Skorupski, belonged to yet another order, the *Ka-dam pa*, prominent in Tibet and Ladakh in the eleventh century.[8] It is, however, no longer active.

It is as yet not possible to tell to which order the majority of the people of Ladakh belong. Suffice it to say that such divisions are not strictly maintained. That is, should it be that a *Duk-pa* lama were performing a ritual, it would be unheard of for a layman, say of the *Gelugs-pa* order, not to regard it reverently.

57

*Young Ladakhi women in their finery for a festival.*

Nor are villages divided strictly along sectarian lines. More often than not, a village will have adherents of both orders.

We have seen that the clergy is invited to participate on such occasions as marriage, birth and death. In addition, no important event is undertaken without first consulting a lama. When a house is built, the lama is asked to perform a ritual appeasing the spirits that dwell where the house is going to be built, and to pray for the success of the family building the house. When it is time to begin harvesting, a prayer of thanksgiving is offered. And each day is begun with the lighting of the oil lamp before the family altar. Invariably each household will have a small *lha-khang*, or chapel, where lamas are invited each month to perform special prayers for protection and the happiness of the family concerned.

This then is the pervading spirit of Buddhism, a heart-warming one indeed, and one which is still wide spread in Ladakh. It is this spirit that has built the magnificient monasteries which have earned Ladakh the description of "land of monasteries". That it is an *attitude* which has created these monasteries is important to remember; especially at the present time when feelings regarding the deterioration of these structures and tourist curiosity about them run high. It is true that the monasteries must be kept up, but it is more important for the visitor to Ladakh, indeed for Ladakhis themselves, to appreciate the mental and spiritual framework which has given birth to the monastery. The continuance of this tradition is the only condition which will truly "preserve" these structures, and Ladakh, as well.

The circumstances regarding the first influx of Islam into Ladakh are, as yet, an uninvestigated field. Theoretically, Islam could have been introduced in the region as early as the late fourteenth century, when Kashmir had just been Islamicised by the Mughal rulers. A century about which a little more is known, however, is the sixteenth when, as has already been seen, Mirza Haidar Dughlat came from Central Asia and converted the region known as Baltistan to Islam. This Islamic momentum was carried as far east as Kargil, one of the districts within Ladakh.

It might be said that there are in general two kinds of Muslims in Ladakh. The first, and by far the larger number, are the Muslims who were converted by Mirza Haidar Dughlat and are known as the Balti. These Muslims were a Tibetan-speaking people from ancient times. While most of them live within what is now Pakistan, the people who inhabit the Kargil area in Ladakh are also known as Balti, as are the Muslims of the Suru valley to the south of Kargil. The Balti are Shi'i Muslims.

The other Muslim group in Ladakh is known as *arghun*. These are the descendants of early Muslim missionaries and traders from the Kashmir valley. These traders and missionaries married women of Tibetan stock who converted to Islam. Their offspring are also known as *arghun*. In contrast to the Balti, the *arghun* are Sunni Muslims. They live mostly in the main Indus valley around Leh, although they are found in Zangskar as well.[9] While the Balti are primarily an agricultural people, the *arghun* have customarily taken to trade.

Over the years the Muslims and the Buddhists have lived in admirable harmony with each other. While there have been instances of Muslims converting to Buddhism and Buddhists converting to Islam, the two communities by and large have kept to themselves. Mutual respect for each other's religion has not, however, suffered. On Muslim festive occasions, Buddhist friends come to offer congratulations and *vice versa*. This is true in the case of the Christian Ladakhis as well. There are many instances of such sharing. In present day Leh, for example, during the month of *ramadhan*, when Muslims fast from dawn to dusk, a special arrangement is made so that electric light, which is normally available only for three hours at night, is made available for the pre-dawn meal. This is particularly striking when it is considered that the Muslims are in the minority in Leh. Similarly, in days gone by, it was a Muslim family which carried a nominal tribute from the Ladakh region to the Dalai Lama in Lhasa.

In most villages or towns with a sizeable Muslim population there is a mosque. As anywhere else, prayer-calls five times a day can be heard from the minarets, and on Fridays the traditional congregation of the faithful is held. During the long winter days the attendance at the mosques increases noticeably, for the Ladakhi Muslim has learned the technique of the *hamam* from the Kashmir valley. This is a method whereby the basement of a portion of the mosque is heated by a wood fire. This in turn serves to heat water for the ritual ablutions as well. Numerous must be the occasions when the high attendance at this only "centrally heated" place in a town or village has been interpreted as an instance of religious zeal!

Until about fifty years ago, the literary language of the Muslims in Ladakh was Persian. Recently this has been replaced by Urdu. The spoken language for the Ladakhi Muslims has always been Ladakhi and still is. This is not to say that no Muslims can be found who can read and write Tibetan, or no Buddhist to read Urdu.

Another faith that is substantially represented in Ladakh is Christianity. Christian missionaries who came to the Tibetan-speaking areas were sent relatively early – as far back as the early seventeenth century. First to come were Catholic missionaries, people like Father Antonio d'Andrade and Father Ippolito Desideri of the Jesuits. These missions were, however, headed for Central Tibetan lands and though Desideri spent a summer in Leh learning the language, he did not establish a mission there. He, and d'Andrade, a Portuguese, were not successful in their attempts to convert the Tibetans.

The branch of Christianity which was successful was the Moravian Church. At its headquarters the Moravian Church had designated the Himalayas as Mission District No. 13.[10] Ladakh was included in this district and the spreading of the Gospels began in 1853. The missionaries who came to Ladakh learned much about their mission district and are considered the pioneers in the study of the language, history and civilization of Ladakh. In turn they taught the Gospels in a manner which did not interfere with the general flow of the everyday life of their converts. Indeed, days like Christmas are celebrated with a distinctly Ladakhi flavour and carol singing on Christmas Eve in a valley with 18,000 foot peaks dominating it can be a scene to move any heart.

There are not many Ladakhi Christians but the people of this community have produced doctors, engineers, writers and scholars far exceeding their proportion in Ladakh. Indeed, the Ladakhi Christians are the first community in the region to have met the challenge of the modern world and have therefore been able to cushion themselves against some of its excesses. They have churches conducting regular services in Leh, Sheh and Khalatse.

Ladakh's proudest boast today is its legacy of harmonious existence between the three religious communities that are represented in the region. There are some signs that this legacy is starting to crumble, and perhaps the greatest gift that the people of Ladakh can give themselves for the future is to ensure that this does not happen.

# Footnotes to The Present

[1] That is, the "Dark Age", or the last one in the eternal cycle of time.

[2] See, AN ACCOUNT OF TIBET: THE TRAVELS OF IPPOLITO DESIDERI, by Father Ippolito Desideri (Edited by Filippo de Filippi), George Routledge & Sons Ltd., London, 1931, 1937, p. 186.

[3] Monks in general are called TABA; a LAMA is a "superior" monk: that is, one who has passed certain examinations so as to deserve the title.

[4] Each individual monastery slightly differs in how it conducts its festivities. The description given above is a synthesized version of several of these. Some monasteries are also visited by Deities, called LHA, during the festival. This is done through the medium of the oracles.

[5] Buddhists cremate their dead, usually at the edges of the village. Muslim and Christian Ladakhis, of course, resort to burial.

[6] This term should not be construed to be derogatory. The same expression could be used in the case of Founders and Saints of other traditions. Historical fact, it should be remembered, does not constitute a value in and of itself; whereas at the same time, a "legendary" narrative is not necessarily devoid of the ability to impart truth. Therein lies its value.

[7] Milarepa's poetry and biography make perhaps the most delightful of readings about Tibetan civilization even in translation. An English version, edited by W.Y. Evans-Wentz, entitled MILAREPA, TIBET'S GREAT YOGI, London 1951 and a French translation by J. Bacot entitled LE POÈTE TIBÉTAIN MILAREPA, Paris, 1925 might be read with profit and pleasure.

[8] Other orders are also represented in Ladakh. But for the sake of clarity and brevity, only the major orders have been mentioned so as to avoid confusing the reader.

[9] We are, of course, dealing in generalities here. Pockets of either group can be found in other areas as well.

[10] Cf., Sven Hedin, TRANS-HIMALAYA, Vol. III, Macmillian & Co., London, 1913, p. 377.

*A Ladakhi shepherd wearing his warmest clothes against the winter cold.*

Faces of Ladakh. Top left: Young women wrapped in sheepskin capes watching a festival from beneath the banners. Far left, bottom: A young Ladakhi boy. Centre left: A young mother and child. They are arghun, descendants of early Muslim missionaries and traders from the Kashmir Valley who married women of Tibetan stock who converted to Islam. Above left centre: A young monk in ceremonial dress. Above right centre: An old woman, moved to tears as she prays when the great scroll is unrolled. Right: A Tibetan refugee from Chang-thang fingers his prayer beads. Below: Young spectators at a festival.

# THE FUTURE

Not more than fifty years ago Leh was an important trade entrepot for Central Asian commerce. Many a traveller of that period described how the bazaar in the town was gradually transformed at the approach of the summer months. Traders and merchants from both north and south congregated here, informing, negotiating and doing business with the authorities of the land. To the market-place Ladakhis brought the famous *pashmina* wool, Yarkandis displayed their grand carpets, Tibetans carried brick-tea and Kashmiris brought in spices and goods made in British India.

In the fourth decade of this century trade with Sinkiang came to a halt because of the political changes there. In the following decade, commercial relations with Tibet came to a dead end for similar reasons when the People's Republic of China occupied Tibet. Much of the exchange with the Kashmir valley also disappeared as the goods brought from there could no longer be sent on to Central Asian and Tibetan territories. Ladakh had lost its place as a trade mart.

In 1962 Ladakh regained its importance but this time for different reasons. The People's Republic of China, it became apparent, had entrenched itself in Indian territory on the Aksai Chin and the eyes of the world were riveted on India's Himalayan province as the two nations fought a rapid war which has ever since been a thorn in the side of relations between them. Following the war, the need to strengthen Indian defence in the region became obvious and there was a sizeable troop build-up in Ladakh. The area was also designated militarily sensitive and closed to non-Indians.

This policy of excluding foreigners from Ladakh came to an end in 1974. In the autumn of that year it was thrown open to the rapidly growing world tourist industry, and ever since, the tourist influx into Ladakh has increased by leaps and bounds during the summer months. In 1979 alone there were nearly 10,000 tourists who visited Ladakh. Almost overnight tourism has become the most lucrative business for a Ladakhi.

Any discussion about the future of Ladakh must take into consideration these developments; namely, the elimination of Ladakh's prominence as an ancient trade centre, its re-emergence as a strategically important area for India and the introduction of tourism. As a centre for the old system of trading, Ladakh could afford to dictate to her visitors her own terms. More so because visitors were not overwhelming in number and they could and did

65

*Men and women gossip and bargain at the temporary bazaar*
*that has sprung up during the Thikse festival.*

conform to the ways of the host culture as much as possible. As part of a modern nation-state, the degree of autonomy has been reduced, since the concept of the nation-state, by definition, attempts to benefit "the larger number". But India is a democracy and by virtue of this fact it pledged to protect the interests of its minorities. It is to this provision that the Ladakhis cling for their future survival as a thriving culture within India's multi-faceted family.

For those sympathetic to the way of life in Ladakh, it is encouraging to see that still the prayer-wheel is spun, the call to prayer heard from the minarets of the mosque, and the village craftsman patronised by the people. Such activities are common even in a place like Leh, which is perhaps the most changed area in Ladakh. And not far away from Leh, in the village of Thikse, there is enough fervour for tradition today to permit the monastery there to build a grand new temple with a huge statue of Maitreya, the Buddha of the future, using traditional art and architectural motifs.

The future then, appears to be secure, for if this direction is maintained, it is not impossible that the traditional personality of the people of the land will continue to show itself in spite of the inevitable changes that are imminent. But the symptoms are not, it must be admitted, always so bright. When talking to Ladakhis, particularly of the younger generation, it is often possible to sense an urgency on their part to understand the world outside. This is a natural tendency and to a certain extent it must be encouraged, but at the same time it ought to be clearly seen that Ladakhis cannot afford to comprehend the world at large *at the expense of* an understanding of their own environment. This betrayal of traditions is to be observed in such statements as "Such and such an attitude is wrong because it is not modern" or "Ladakhis must change to suit the times". Ladakhis cannot but be who they are. To betray this identity in order to fall in with the times would be to invite the extinction of their culture.

The reader must not be misled. There is much discussion, both among Ladakhis as well as non-Ladakhis, as to the need to "preserve" Ladakh. But the term comes too close to relegating Ladakh to a place in the museum of a "brave new world". The need is not so much to "preserve" but to understand. Ladakh must be understood for what it is and if this is done the future will take care of itself.

If the reader interprets what has just been said as a sentimental yearning for the past, he is again being unintentionally misled. Indeed, the present writer's thesis is that the Ladakh of the past has not "gone by". It is very much alive and to understand it better, what is needed is not so much sentiment as practicality. The few changes, such as the presence of army bases and the introduction of tourism, have come about as a result of historical circumstances. These developments need not be sentimentally lamented if properly understood. For instance, it has become almost fashionable to criticise the

66

presence of the Indian Army in Ladakh as a negative influence on the landscape! This approach is evidently silly when it is considered that the country can hardly afford to leave its frontiers unprotected. If such neglect were followed up, there would be very little left to "preserve", if the fate of Buddhism in Tibet is anything to go by. In addition, very often the casual observer does not remark that the Indian Army is a self-contained institution and that its social and economic impact on the region is minimal.

The issue of tourism is a much more complex one. It was introduced at the request of Ladakhis themselves who saw in it a means for earning extra income. For India as a whole, the tourist industry is a means for earning much needed foreign exchange. Hence tourism is encouraged both at the regional as well as the national level, giving it a fairly definite place. Thus, tourism cannot be unilaterally eliminated by those who see and anticipate some of its negative by-products.

But at the same time, nothing is more startling in its effects on Ladakh, and Leh in particular, than the demands of tourism. The quantity of "antiques" has soared in the past few years, taxi fares are among the highest in India and the number of "hotels" in Leh rivals that of Srinagar, a long established tourist town. The need then is to see that the industry is channelled in such a way that its potential evils are lessened. This is a particularly complex task because tourism in Ladakh represents a point of contact between two different systems of values. Therefore it requires alertness both on the part of the Ladakhi and the overwhelmingly western visitors to his land. Often even the well-meaning visitor will do more harm than he ever intends to, as the following incident will illustrate.

Not long ago I was involved in a discussion between a western architect and a Ladakhi mason. My rôle was that of interpreter. As the discussion progressed, the architect wondered about a feature of Ladakhi house construction which caused the walls to lean inwards so that the base was wider than the roof. He was intrigued by the aesthetic effect of this feature and wanted to reproduce it, with an angle somewhat more acute than usual. The mason proceeded to attempt this but was unsuccessful, whereupon the architect was inclined to criticise the mason's incompetence. What my western friend failed to grasp was that the mason produced houses to live in, *not* for *aesthetic* enjoyment! Whatever aesthetic qualities a finished product possesses are quite incidental to the aim of the Ladakhi craftsman. At most it is a by-product of his devotion to his aim of constructing a worthy dwelling place. By imposing his own "purely aesthetic" and "art for art's sake" values on the mason, the architect was engaged in an intellectual colonialism which is more dangerous than anything the Ladakhi has yet experienced. More so the danger because the architect did not recognise his deep seated prejudices.

In a more concrete vein, the future of Ladakh depends on the children of Ladakh. It is clear, therefore, that extreme care must be taken to ensure that they are given an education which will properly develop their whole character and not merely teach them book knowledge. The task of doing this lies with the Ladakhi schools, of which there are many.

In these schools the children learn the basics of a literate society. In addition to reading, writing and arithmetic, the children are taught English, Urdu and Tibetan. Like most of the world over, the education is undergoing scrutiny in India as well. The problem is one of avoiding an over-estimation of the need for a so-called "modern education" for the children. It cannot be denied, and such is not the intention here, that teaching the child how to acquire the basics of literacy is important in this day and age. But in a society such as Ladakh's, extreme care must be taken to ascertain that a "literate" individual is not created at the cost of the same individual not being equipped to function as a member of his community and environment. In India a step in this direction has been taken by ensuring that the schools teach the local language of the area. Hence, Ladakhi children continue to learn their own language, thereby lessening the risk of alienation from their surroundings.

Once he has left the school, the young educated Ladakhi is again exposed to a whole new vocabulary. Words like "development", "progress" and "alternative technology" are commonplace ones that he is likely to hear. It is imperative that such terminology be carefully examined and redefined or even rejected if necessary; for it behoves the Ladakhi to make certain that when he is dealing with the future of his culture, he is doing so with an awareness of its past. He must define terms in the light of such an awareness and his own Ladakhi-ness.

It must not be said that no one, least of all the Ladakhis, cared.

*A large painted scroll, or* thanka, *is unveiled at the beginning of the festival at Thikse monastery. The scrolls are made of silk, covered with brocade veils. They are only revealed once every year, and are prized as the monastery's most valuable possession. They show Buddha flanked by his attendants.*

Following double page: The expenses for the monastery festivals are borne by laymen, whose only reward is the blessing from the head lama. At Thikse monastery, the sponsors, holding white ceremonial scarves called kha-dags, gather before the courtyard altar of the head lama to receive his blessings.

*Monks blow the long copper trumpets on the rooftop of Thikse monastery, filling the valley below with their mournful sound.*

70

*A lama recites prayers and reads from the Kanjur, the revealed texts, accompanied by the cymbal and drum, in a monthly prayer ceremony for a Ladakhi family.*

Ladakhi religious festivals: Top left: A costumed dancer at the Hemis festival, one of the few Buddhist festivals to be held in the summer. Top centre: The masked dancers, representing saints and gods in the Tibetan Buddhist pantheon, enter the courtyard of Thikse monastery from the main assembly hall, the Dhu-khang. Left: Monks masked as skeletons perform a frenzied dance before their entrance to the courtyard for the mystery play at Likir monastery. Above: Young masked monks beg for sweets and joke with the spectators before the more serious masked dances. Right: A masked dancer at Thikse monastery.

*Masked dancers at Likir monastery. The dancing master, who acts as master of ceremonies, stands on the right of the line holding ribbons.*

*Villagers at Stok bow low in submission as the Lha passes. Lhas are local villagers believed to be possessed by a divinity, and who, after a period of abstinence, go into a trance. The trance may be so intense that they inflict wounds on themselves, although their attendants are supposed to prevent this. They may also act as oracles when possessed, and villagers timidly offer them white scarves in the hopes of a revelation. Following double page: The Lhas climb on the narrow roof parapet high above Stok monastery courtyard, and shout defiance to the crowd below.*

*An anguished Lha draws the blade of his sword across his tongue.*

*Sword and standard raised above his head, a Lha dashes wildly through
the courtyard past masked dancers going through their steps.*

80

*The Likir festival. Monks crowd the steps of the
monastery library for a view of the mystery play.*

*Monks of the Yellow Hat,* Gelugs-pa *order, herald
the unfurling of the large* Thanka *scroll at Likir.*

*Members of a Ladakhi family, young and old alike, gather round a* lama *and his attendant monk on the roof of their home. The* lama *holds a bell and sceptre in one hand, the holy water pitcher in the other, as he prepares for the* Chaptus *ceremony, a ritual of purification.*

*A Ladakhi pilgrim to Likir turns a prayer wheel. Inscribed on the outside, and printed thousands of times on the long ribbons coiled inside are the sacred words "Om! Mani Padme Hum!" Buddhists hold that the repetition of the sacred text enables them to acquire merit. By spinning the wheel, the text passes before the individual and works its effect.*

*The traditional symbols of wisdom: the bell* (Dril-bu) *and the sceptre* (Dorje).

*The head of Maitreya, the future Buddha, in Sum-tsek Temple. The entire figure stands nearly fifteen feet tall, and is one of three Bodhisattva images in alcoves within the Temple.*

*Influences from west Central Asia and Mughal India are evident in this detail of a battle scene depicted on a thanka at Alchi. The background design – pine trees – also suggests Chinese influence.*

*A mandala, Sum-tsek Temple, dating from about the tenth-eleventh centuries.*

*The Goddess Perfection of Wisdom, Sum-tsek Temple.*

*Modern religious painting adorning Stok monastery.*

*Paintings decorating the walls at the entrance to the main* Gompa, *Thikse.*

*A modern decoration over a column in Stok monastery.*

94

*Kashmiri influence is reflected in a carved column and the façade of Sum-tsek Temple, Alchi.*

*Pages from the books of the tradition, called the Kanjur and the Tangyur. The former are the revealed texts, the latter the commentaries. The lama brings the book to the people, reading from it and expounding the texts.*

# THE TOURIST IN LADAKH

Tourism is one of the world's largest industries and it continues to grow each year. Ladakh, since late 1974, has experienced a heavy dose of the tourist trade and it is not unlikely that this traffic will increase as time passes. It is appropriate, therefore, that we examine, however briefly, the impact of this phenomenon in Ladakh and furnish our readers with some information on the practical aspects of a visit to the region.

To begin with, it is hoped that those who visit Ladakh will come away with an "educational" experience in the fullest sense of the word. While being involved in the tourist industry for the past year, I took the opportunity of asking several tourists what it was that attracted them to Ladakh, or to tour in general. Inevitably, part of the answer was "to understand other cultures and ways of life". This is indeed a noble aim if the words "to understand" mean not mere satisfaction of curiosity but the internalisation of the experience to such an extent that it affects the intellectual perspective on the world at large. Indeed, in so doing the modern tourist will at least in part be emulating the "tourists" of an earlier time, then known as pilgrims, who visited shrines and holy places in order to gain knowledge and merit.

It may not be apparent to someone who has not been to Ladakh prior to 1974, but places like Leh have undergone a tremendous change since then. The number of shops has increased by as much as 100 per cent, sanitation has become one of the worst problems, and increasingly the tourist demands are being catered for at the expense of the needs of the Ladakhis. While there are the usual "pro-tourism" arguments of the sociologist, such as the increase in the per capita income of the people, the availability of a larger variety of commodities to Ladakhis and so forth, what we wish to point out is that there is such a thing as bad tourism and that unfortunately this is easier to provide for than "good" tourism. At its core, bad tourism is aimed at exploiting the natural beauty and cultural heritage of a region for quick

97

financial gains without respect or concern for the social, ecological or intellectual prerogatives of the host culture*. It is the unqualified responsibility of the tour operator to endeavour to minimize such negative effects upon Ladakh or, for that matter, any other culture to which they bring their clients.

The client, or the tourist, also has a responsibility in this debate regarding positive versus negative tourism. First, he should try to choose a tour operator who is responsible in his attitude towards the host culture. He should endeavour to see beyond the advertisements that promise a journey to "exotic" or "untouched regions" and observe whether the tour operator has high standards regarding, for example, the ecology; does he clean up properly after using a camp-site? Next, the tourist should try to find out as much as he can about Ladakh before going there, both through books and orientation programmes that tour operators could and should provide. Too often there is a tendency to unthinkingly hand out pens, sweets or, worse, money, to little children who appear to the casual observer to be "poor" and "needy". In parts of Ladakh a visitor may often hear the children or even adults asking for them. This situation, however, distorts not only the visitors' image of Ladakhis, but the Ladakhis' image of visitors as well. The former are tending more and more to view the society as a beggar society and the latter are viewing the foreign visitor as a source of money and trinkets. Money or gifts should be given as an exchange for something and not with a view to providing charitable contributions.

While these thoughts may seem obvious to our readers, the relative infancy of the tourist industry in Ladakh tends to cloud the vision of both Ladakhis and their guests. What should be borne in mind is that because of the late introduction that Ladakh has had to the modern world, the rate of acceleration of the changes taking place is very high and often there is little time to contemplate whether certain changes should take place, how they should be introduced and what the future holds in view of these changes. Activities that are planned either by or for the visitor to Ladakh must have these facts as a guide. In addition to visits to the monasteries, palaces and citadels of Ladakh, itineraries should include opportunities for observing the Ladakhi way of life; for it is the attitude which governs the latter which has created the spectacles that most tourists come to Ladakh to see. The tourist must feel an obligation towards Ladakhis to understand their way of life just as the Ladakhis must feel obliged to understand that of their guests. It is the only way in which a "fair" exchange can take place and which will contribute to a better understanding by both the parties involved.

---

*While this may seem like a strange statement to make, it is not when we consider that "too much concern" for the host culture may tend to cut into the profits of a business and increase its overhead.

# Getting to Ladakh

Leh, the principal township of Ladakh, is a little over 400 kilometres from Srinagar, the capital of Jammu and Kashmir State. There are three ways in which to travel to Leh. First, by a thirty-five minute plane flight on Indian Airlines from Srinagar. (It is also possible to fly directly from New Delhi on the same day although the plane makes a stop in Srinagar for an hour or so.) This is a truly spectacular flight giving the passengers a view of the mightiest mountain ranges in the world including the Pir Panjal Range, the Karakorum Mountains, the Great Himalaya Range, the Zangskar Range and the Ladakh Range. However, the disadvantage of this approach is that it does not give an opportunity to acclimatise and the first couple of days in Leh after arriving by air could be accompanied by headache and nausea. It is generally recommended that flying be chosen as a means of exit rather than entry into the country.

The second, and most desirable, way of coming to Ladakh is by trekking. This mode gives the traveller not only an excellent chance to acclimatise but provides him with an excellent visual and cultural introduction to Ladakh as well. We have included tips for the prospective trekker later in this chapter.

The third approach is by a two day bus or jeep journey along a surfaced road. This road was begun in the first half of this century and was strengthened after the 1962 war primarily for defence purposes. For most of the way this road follows the traditional trade route between Srinagar and Leh, thus giving modern travellers a glimpse of many villages which are historically and culturally important. Perhaps the most dramatic part of this journey is the ascent up the Zoji-La or Zoji Pass. As the traveller winds up this road, he sees the hills are covered with evergreen trees and shrubs. The final turn at the head of the Zoji-La introduces the visitor to the Ladakhi landscape. Before him is a vast mountain desert dotted with oases which receive their nourishment from rivers, streams and springs. The first group of villages encountered from Dras to Kargil approximate to the area which is largely inhabited by Ladakhi Muslims. This part of the journey is governed mostly by the Dras and Wakha Rivers. From Kargil, where travellers rest for the night, the next stage consists of a climb over two major passes, Namika-La and Fotu-La, to arrive in Leh in the evening. Along the way the route passes through some important sites such as the villages of Khalatse where a rebellion against the Dogra ruler in Ladakh met with defeat in the winter of 1841–42; Mulbekh where there can be seen a huge rock carving of Maitreya; Lamayuru with its famous monastery and Basgo with its fortress, the site of a three year siege in the late seventeenth century when a Tibeto-Mongol army invaded Ladakh.

# Tourist Accommodation in Ladakh

The novelty of tourism in the region must be taken into consideration when planning accommodation in Ladakh. For the obvious reasons of difficulties of transport and access there are certain limitations and the kind of facilities that would be available in a more established tourist area cannot be expected. However, there are several hotels and guest houses in Leh, and some others in villages surrounding it.

# Activities

Itineraries in Ladakh can range from exclusive tours to the monasteries to trekking to the villages. In addition, a museum opened in the Palace at Stok in June, 1980 and the more ambitious tourist may want to visit the School of Buddhist Philosophy at Choglamsar or the office of the Cultural Academy of Jammu and Kashmir State which has a wing in Leh to help promote the study of Ladakhi culture.

The monasteries that might be visited in addition to Lamayuru include the eleventh century monastery of Alchi on the Srinagar-Leh road, Hemis, Sheh, Thikse, Phyang and Spituk. It is advisable, however, that unless the tourist has a specific interest in visiting monasteries, he should visit just two or three of those mentioned. There are, of course, many more monasteries. Sheh also has the ruins of an old fortress. In Leh itself there is the early sixteenth century temple of the Guardian Divinities, or *gon-khang*, crowning the peak to the north-east of the town. This peak is called Namgyal Peak. The fort-like palace which dominates Leh was built in the early part of the seventeenth century and this too can be visited, although it is also in ruins.

It is highly recommended that during their stay in Ladakh visitors take a day's walk to a village near Leh. This will give them an opportunity to observe the everyday activities of Ladakhis first hand and should they be invited into a house for a cup of tea or *chang* it will give them a chance to see how Ladakhis live as well. A walk in the village might also provide an opportunity to see the village craftsman at work or if the visit happens to be in the summer months, there might be an archery contest. In the winter months there are several festivals held by the various monasteries.

100

# The Land and Trekking by Kenneth R. Storm, Jr.

The landscapes of Ladakh at times seem to belong more to a realm of the imagination than to the physical world. All the familiar elements of a landscape are here, mountains, valleys, rivers and plains, but in Ladakh these are often found in unexpected combinations, delighting the eye by their dramatic contrasts. Rocky defiles of awesome proportion border broad valleys cut by lazy rivers; dry, limitless expanses of rock devoid of all vegetation merge suddenly with moist, upland meadows, richly carpeted with grasses and alpine flowers.

Any traveller who visits Ladakh will spend much of his time in the Indus Valley, probably at Leh. Climb to the palace above the city, or higher, to Namgyal Peak, and look out across the valley to the south. There is plenty of room here. The eye can wander freely for miles following the sloping terrace upward from the river, past the village of Stok, to the lifeless, furrowed face of the Zangskar Mountains. Higher still, at over 20,000 feet above sea level, Stok Kangri or "Stok Mountain" lifts its head above the other un-named peaks. Its slopes are draped with snow the year round. The lack of vegetation is unsettling at first, but soon the mind adjusts and seeks comfort in fields of barley climbing a distant mountainside and in the sky of deep blue. In all, there is a comfortable sense of proportion to the landscape in the Indus Valley. Certainly there is nothing to suggest that what lies beyond, in the Zangskar Mountains, belongs to another world.

For a short hike into the Zangskar Range follow the streams into the mountains above the villages of Matho or Stok. Beyond the first bend a wall of rock rises abruptly cutting off the Indus Valley. There are no more sweeping views. You are a prisoner now in the heart of mountains that grow wilder with each step. Nature has lost control. Rocks deposited on ancient sea floors have been broken and uplifted to vertical walls, some thousands of feet high. Everything seems to hang in a precarious balance threatening to crash down upon you at any instant. Three to four hours' march later, around another bend, the scene changes again. The immense walls of the gorge pull back. The mountains continue to rise but now with gentle, rounded shoulders, to meet the snow-covered heights. There are shepherds' huts among the boulders, and if you are here in mid-summer there is a cast of green on the hillsides.

Trekking in Ladakh, whether for a single day or for several weeks, can be a rewarding experience. Once you leave the Indus Valley however, it is not enough to be in top physical condition; you must also be extremely well prepared to face the rigors of backcountry travel. (See equipment list.)

Keep in mind that the conditions found in Ladakh, both desert and arctic, are found in very few other places on earth. Add to this Ladakh's extreme elevation, everywhere above 10,000 feet, and the problems compound. Proper acclimatisation is the biggest concern. On a trek I met a young man staggering along the track, pale and obviously quite ill. He had arrived in Leh from New Delhi by plane two days before and had attempted a pass above 16,000 feet. He explained that he had considerable Alpine experience and had trained several weeks for the trip at home. In his enthusiasm he was certain his conditioning would compensate for the quick trip up from near sea level. He learned a very painful lesson. Acclimatisation need not be a problem. Give yourself several leisurely days of sightseeing and shopping in Leh and visiting the Indus Valley before beginning a trek. Begin with short hikes before you attempt the longer, more difficult routes.

Be aware of changing conditions from season to season. In May and early June snow often lies deep on the high passes making travel difficult to impossible, while by July and August snowmelt swells most of the mountain streams making icy crossings frequent and treacherous. Ladakhis often designate tracks as summer or winter routes depending on the water level. The autumn is an ideal time of year for trekking in Ladakh. Most of the streams subside by late September and the winter snows do not fall until November. Winter trekking is becoming more popular. For those hardy enough to brave the cold temperatures, the experience of hiking along the frozen surface of a river, such as the Zangskar, through gorges thousands of feet deep, is unsurpassed.

In Leh there are a limited number of outfitters able to supply some equipment (tents, sleeping bags, jackets), maps, guides and pack animals. If you travel on your own make sure you have accurate information. The journals and books of nineteenth century explorers in Ladakh, such as Thomas Thomson, often provide useful and exciting itineraries for treks. With a little research and planning, treks can take on expeditionary aspects. For example, Ladakh may be reached on foot from Manali (in the Indian state of Himachal Pradesh) crossing the Great Himalaya Range into the upper Zangskar Valley, along tracks in use for centuries.

Trekkers are advised to carry as much of their own food as possible. Some supplies may be purchased from villagers along the way, but remember, Ladakh is a harsh land and most people cannot afford to sell valuable stocks of grain set aside for the long winter.

The tourist in Ladakh is not free to roam anywhere he pleases. The government of India has restricted travel north of a line one mile north of the Indus River (with the exception of a few villages) and in the Indus Valley beginning just east of Hemis Monastery. The Ladakh Range behind Leh is forbidden to trekkers.

# What to Bring

While the visitor is in Ladakh he is at an average elevation of 11,000 feet above sea level. The air at this altitude is rarefied and very dry, the average annual rainfall being barely three to four inches. During the summer months, that is, early June to the end of August, the days are warm (70 to 80 degrees F) and the evenings cold (45 degrees F or less). During the other months travellers should bring winter clothing. Below is a list of the various things the traveller should bring with him. A list of additional items for the person who plans on trekking is also provided.

*General Items:*

Wool sweater
Down jacket (light)
Shoes, boots (sturdy pair for walking)
Day pack
Hat (wide-brimmed)

Sleeping bag
Sunglasses
Sunscreen lotion
Skin creme
Lip salve
Flashlight, candles

Trekkers will need these additional items:

Boots (heavy duty)
Wool socks (several pairs)
Moleskin (for blisters)
Balaclava
Gloves, mittens
Long underwear
Wool pants
Down jacket (heavy)
Wind parka
Rain gear

Tent
Insulated ground pad

Sleeping bag (heavy-duty)

Backpack

Kerosene stove
Spare fuel bottle
Cooking equipment
(pots, cup, utensils, etc.)
Canteens
Water purification tablets
Freeze-dried food

First aid kit

(Optional summer items; recommended in winter)

Ice axe
Snow goggles
Gaiters

# A Note on Photography by Kenneth R. Storm, Jr.

The photographer in Ladakh should be prepared for problems unique to this region of low rainfall, extremes in temperature, and high altitude. With vegetation limited to the watercourses and irrigated fields, there is little to hold the soil, which throughout much of Ladakh is granite weathered to a fine powder. Winds are often strong during the summer months, driving a film of dust into unprotected cameras. To avoid jamming the mechanisms or a costly cleaning job when you return home, cameras and lenses should be stored in "zip-lock" plastic bags whenever they are not in use. If you are planning a winter trip to Ladakh, you might consider having your camera winterised. Although daytime temperatures in the winter may rise above freezing, at night, or at higher elevations, the temperature frequently falls well below zero degrees F. Spare batteries for the light meter are a must.

Camera equipment and film are obviously areas of personal preference. Since I like to carry my own equipment on my back when trekking, compactness and lightweight, in addition to quality, were important factors in my choice of a camera and lenses. I use a 35 mm SLR, Nikon FM, with several Nikkor lenses ranging from 24 mm to 200 mm. For this book I used primarily Kodachrome 25 and 64 film. Indoors, I prefer to shoot in available light whenever possible. For these situations I rely on Ektachrome 400 film and a small tripod. I find a polarizing filter valuable in reducing glare and reflections, especially from bare rock. Flash photography is often prohibited within certain sections of monasteries, so use a flash with discretion and ask permission. Most important of all, bring plenty of film: I suggest at least twice as much as you would normally expect to use on a trip. Judging from the many tourists I met who asked me for extra rolls of film after exhausting their own supply in three days, unexposed film is a rare commodity in Ladakh!

104

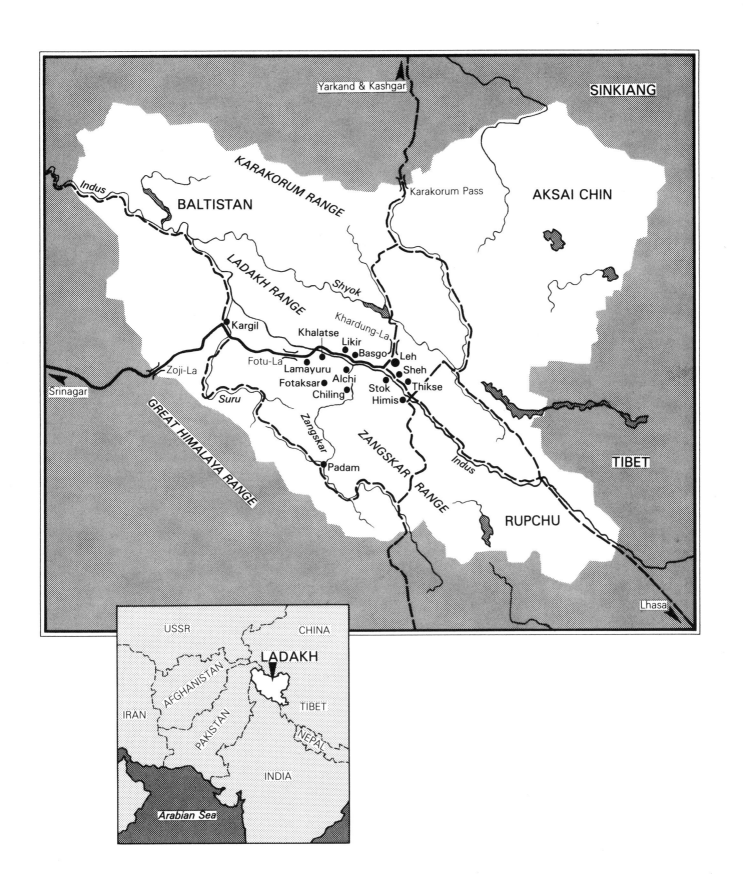

# BIBLIOGRAPHY

Ahmed, Z. "Tibet and Ladakh: A History" in FAR EASTERN AFFAIRS, Number 3, London 1963, pp. 23–58.

Desideri, I. AN ACCOUNT OF TIBET (edited by Filippo de Filippi), George Routledge and Sons, Ltd., London, 1931, 1937.

Francke, A. H. A HISTORY OF WESTERN TIBET, London, 1906.

Hedin, S. TRANS-HIMALAYA: Discoveries and Adventures in Tibet, Macmillan and Co., 1909, 3 Vols. Vol III, 1913.

Snellgrove, D.L. and Skorupski, Taduez. THE CULTURAL HERITAGE OF LADAKH, Prajna Press, Boulder, 1977.

In addition to the above sources, we should like to suggest the following books to the reader interested in continuing his readings on Ladakh and Tibetan civilisation in general.

HIMALAYAN BATTLEGROUND by M. Fisher, L. Rose and R. Huttenback (London, 1963) gives a good account of the recent history of the region. Alistair Lamb's BRITAIN AND CHINESE CENTRAL ASIA (London, 1960) is a book in the same category giving the commercial history of the area up to 1905.

LAND AND POLITY IN TIBET by P. Carrasco (Seattle, 1959) has an excellent summary of the socio-political make-up of Himalayan States, including a section on Ladakh.

Two books by J. Keay, WHEN MEN AND MOUNTAINS MEET and THE GILGIT GAME, serve as a beautiful introduction to the region through the eyes of the early explorers. For a vivid, sympathetic and highly sensitive personal account of travel in the Himalayas, including Ladakh, we should like to direct our readers to the recently republished work by Marco Pallis entitled PEAKS AND LAMAS (London, 1974).

Photolithos Actual S.A., Bienne
Printed by Weber Couleurs S.A., Bienne
Bound by Maurice Busenhart, Lausanne

Printed in Switzerland